Crossing to Sunlight Revisited

Crossing to Sunlight Revisited

NEW AND SELECTED POEMS

Paul Zimmer

The University of Georgia Press

ATHENS & LONDON

Published by The University of Georgia Press
Athens, Georgia 30602
© 2007 by Paul Zimmer

Set in Monotype Garamond
Printed and bound by Thomson-Shore
The paper in this book meets the guidelines for
permanence and durability of the Committee on
Production Guidelines for Book Longevity of the
Council on Library Resources.

Printed in the United States of America

11   10   09   08   07   P   5   4   3   2   1

Library of Congress Cataloging-in-Publication Data

Zimmer, Paul.
Crossing to sunlight revisited : new and selected poems / Paul Zimmer.
    p. cm.
ISBN-13: 978-0-8203-2944-4 (pbk. : alk. paper)
ISBN-10: 0-8203-2944-4 (pbk. : alk. paper)
I. Title.
PS3576.147C76   2007
811'.54—dc22
2006035804

British Library Cataloging-in-Publication Data available

FOR *Suzanne*

"You live in this, and dwell in lovers' eyes."

Contents

Half a century ago I decided I wanted to be a poet. At
the time, I did not fully realize what a responsibility I was
assuming, but I remain grateful for this decision. Since then
I have tried to work on poems every day. Mostly it has gone
well enough, but there were times when poetry got tangled
in the jobs I was doing to make a living. Even during these
periods, when there were so many other things to do, I kept
working at my lines. Perhaps it is the only courageous thing I
have done in my life, but I remained dogged about poetry.

Now I must admit that I am no longer an aging poet or
an older poet. I am an old poet. It is time to begin measuring
things up for sure. In recent years, for only a brief while,
I considered forming a large, collected volume of my work
but eventually lost interest in this prospect. Such ponderous
books, with their inclusive dates, have always seemed a
bit like tombstones to me. At least in my own case, it did
not seem the best course to follow. Georges Braque once
wrote: "Progress in art does not consist in expanding one's
limitations but in knowing them better."

Here then is a distillation of my poetry, carefully chosen
from a much larger body of writing. I do not feel I am
expanding my limitations as I offer it. It contains twenty-
three new poems from the past decade and fifty older poems
gleaned from my earlier books—a total of seventy-three
poems, one for each of the years I have lived.

PART ONE *Twenty-three New Poems*

Because I Am Heir to Many Things:

warmth of dandelion, shamble of bear,
caution of inchworm, brain of flicker,
I am not surprised when, ankle-deep
in snow among February woods,
I feel suddenly aroused by a sound
like a wooden spoon rattling a bucket.

But it is just another brother, a grouse,
confused and drumming on a hollow log,
like an old man dreaming he is young again,
wishing for love in a preposterous season.

Zimmer Lurches from Chair to Chair,

starts counting on one hand
the minutes he feels good in a day.

Then, as thunderheads gather in
the west, he sees an intruder planted
knee-deep in distant, hovering mist
at the edge of his north forty.

Zimmer thinks to light out after him,
but his legs and breath are gone.

Besides—this is not some
clatter-boned spirit hovering
over the field—but a stranger
standing firm as a knife
thrust into the cold sod.

Zimmer speaks bravely to his body,
addressing it from forehead to toes.
He says, Flesh, you will not be afraid,
you will not pant and grow numb.
Bones, stand with me as always.

But someone is knocking at his door,
puffing cold through the keyhole,
something is turning the knob,
and fear torques Zimmer's ribs.

Three Crows

The year I am ill and down,
Derrie, derrie, downe downe,
Three crows lurk on our lawn.
For months they rattle and caw,
At day's end fly to their roost
With the rest of their murder
To riot as the sun goes down.

Three black boots on our grass,
They linger until snow flies;
Then three black keyholes
Through a leaden door:
One for my breath,
One for my blood,
One for my wounded heart,
With a down derrie
Derrie, derrie, downe downe.

The Moment

As I cross over the rise
I come upon three solemn yearlings
attending the silence.
They hold and stare at me
as if stitched into tapestry.

In these meadows the hush
is medieval and long—
grass draws it up
from dank roots to
sprinkle into sunlight.
There is only birdsong here,
the sibilating leaves,
bees, wasps, dragonflies,
a skirl of crickets
in the tempered wind,
and now the rustle
of three whitetails
slipping off into the trees.

Had it been a hellhound?
Bigfoot come to rampage
In the woods of Wisconsin?
The county paper said
It was "a bear with its hair
Burnt off in a brush fire."

The five of us had dawdled
Too long at our woodcutting.
Now dusk slanted into the trees.

The bear rushed out of
A stand of stricken elms,
This sudden fury
That fell upon us,
This beast that looked
Like a wounded man—
And the moment was combustible,
Blowing apart to lodge in
Different parts of our minds.

"The stink's what I remember,"
Says Eli now. "It rose up like
A dump fire, some high coon
Left by an owl to rot."

Lester shakes his head.
"What raised my hair
Most was that face,
Rawer than a cankered beet."

"It got a paw on me,"
Gus recollects—"cold
As a gravedigger's cock,
And yet it burned me."

"It knocked me down,"
Said Rollo, "and split
My lip. It tasted like
A nest of last year's bees."

But I remember only
The sounds it made,
After we'd heaved
Our firewood at it
And skedaddled.

I looked back to see
It naked and suffering
In the lowering dark,
A demon potent but lost,
Declining into its pain.

"Lester," it rasped at us.
"Gus, Rollo, Eli," as if making
A list to shame us. Then,
"Zimmer," it groaned. I swear.

He might have been no one—
But you could tell he was someone.
What was he looking for that January day
When all of us were yearning for
Even half-light under the graveyard sky?

He wore a hat that looked like a cow pie
When he walked into Burkum's Tap,
Smelling as if he were last year's yeast.
He unstrapped his easel from his back,
Leaned it up against a wall,
And asked for a glass of beer.

Black hair sprouted from his nostrils
Over his mouth and teeth and chin;
He was all cubes, cones, and cylinders.
But those eyes. All you could see were
His eyes. Like an owl's above the dark,
They could make you disappear.

If we had welcomed him to our ridges,
What would he have done with
His dappled hands? Where would
He have stopped, if we had let him start?

But we were afraid of him—the smudges
Of blue and green and orange on
His knuckles, his bluff, unsmiling face.
We pretended he wasn't there, until at last
He gathered up his things and closed
The door behind him as he left.

Stengel calls up and starts spilling us the business.
"I hear you been talking big in Soldiers Grove," he says.
"You got to understand—the Yankees are like
Elephant bulls. We don't take lightly to such talk.
If you girls want a taste of the fire, we can bring it."

"Hell yes!" we say. "Come on in here and find out what
The truth is like." So the whole show comes to Grove.
The American Legion does a fry, the Old Oak Inn books full,
Sports writers come looking for women in Burkum's Tap
Where Mantle is standing drinks for everyone at the bar.
Martin punches the Lutheran minister at a lutefisk supper.
Then there's a little dustup at the community dance.

But when the game begins we start swinging from our heels,
And it's like a meteor shower. Mantle is sliding headfirst through
New manure in the outfield, Bauer trips over the snow fence,
Going for a long one. Berra is wearing a trail to the mound.
Ford, Larsen, Kucks, Turley, Lopat, Grim, Raschi, Reynolds—
The best they had—we gave it back right into their teeth.
By the bottom of the third, Stengel was out of pitchers.
The umpire waved his hands, called the game for mercy.

When it was over, we took it easy on them,
But those slickers had to swallow a lot.
It's all history now, and you could look it up.
We sent them home with their heads in their hands;
We crushed their asses and they never came back.

In Burkum's Tap

Burkum was pitching a fit
At his grill, as I took
My ham and rye at the bar.

Arabs, councilmen, gays—
You name it, he was pissed
Enough at everything to
Outroar the news at noon.

Then he turned his blaze on
The wild boars that folks
Were seeing in stands of oak
Near the township dump.

"Those buggers can lift their heads
And run faster than a man," he said.
"If they take you down,
Your nuts go first; then they
Strip your bones, and blow
Their stink in your face as
They gnaw off your cheeks.

"I seen one the other day and
Gave it all the ground it wanted—
Black as the devil's bunghole,
Tusks like tenpenny nails.

"Who let them suckers loose
Around here? As if
We don't have enough
Trouble in this
Damned world already!"

A Love Poem for Alyce Husar

I am planting trees in a meadow
when I hear a chainsaw
bite into the morning, snarling into
an old oak in my neighbor's woods.

I cut my spade into wet turf
and lift a divot out to see
the dear face of Alyce Husar
like a sleeping toad in the mud,
her eyes unsticking one at a time
as her awareness rises.
At last she is able to focus.
Eighty years old, she says,
"You're going to be mad at me."

In Soldiers Grove a few days
before, I had smashed into
her car broadside when—
with not a blink of caution—she pulled
from her driveway in front of me.

As I helped her out of the street
to the curb, her hand felt chilled,
yet her lovely pearl and gray patina
was glazed and unblemished.

Now at odd, distracting moments,
when I am planting trees
or dozing in my chair,
I recollect what she said next:
"You're going to be mad at me,"
she repeated, then added,
"A lot of people are."

And yes, I was furious
with Alyce Husar,
biting my words back
and ringing my hands
as I stood beside her,
listening to a siren
make its way through
the streets toward us,
but it was a furious love.

Under its eaves are wasps'
and birds' nests in niches,
Spiders circle the sashes.
Other things try to come in—
flies, mosquitoes, dragonflies, ticks.

Winter—scratch of mice, voles,
rabbits gnaw at the siding.

In all weather—sunshine, rain, gloom,
or snow—Zimmer enters with dog,
wind at the door, thermos of tea.

Dog's dish and rug, paper, pencils,
tapes of Basie, Handel, Coleman Hawkins,
small ceramic heater, fan,
weathered books on shelves,
windows that look out on
scribed fields and hills.

Then Zimmer dips down
the groundhog's hole,
Hawkins flies up to the wasps' nest,
groundhog wants the sun's place,
and dog is at the table with her poems.

Bach and My Father

Six days a week my father sold shoes
To support our family through depression and war,
Nursed his wife through years of Parkinson's,
Loved nominal cigars, manhattans, long jokes,
Never kissed me, but always shook my hand.

Once he came to visit me when a Brandenburg
Was on the stereo. He listened with care—
Brisk melodies, symmetry, civility, and passion.
When it finished, he asked to hear it again,
Moving his right hand in time. He would have
Risen to dance if he had known how.

"Beautiful," he said when it was done,
My father, who'd never heard a Brandenburg.
Eighty years old, bent, and scuffed all over,
Just in time he said, "That's beautiful."

William Blake is naked at his sideboard,
talking and singing to himself
as he steeps his morning tea.
Zimmer will pretend to drop down
from a wreath of sorrowing angels,
burst through the roof of Blake's house
like a falling star to prick him
on his left foot and make
his small, taut body
arch back in ecstatic surprise.

Zimmer will pose as Milton, rich
with holy loot, bringing war news
of God and Lucifer, or he'll be
Orc come from America to walk
the bleary streets of London.

Or perhaps he will just be Zimmer,
sitting quietly with the master all day,
listening to the scrape of
his graver and holy ravings,
losing the contest of words again—
great bird of love to tygers of wrath,
big blue train to the giant Albion,
ribs of death to the ancient of days.

But what dim, blunted star,
what fifteen-stone angel,
would care or complain
of losing to William Blake?

One O'clock Jump

Still tingling with Basie's hard cooking,
Between sets Zimmer was standing at the bar
When the man next to him ordered scotch and milk.
Zimmer looked to see who had this stray taste
And almost swooned when he saw the master.

Basie knocked back his shot.
Then when he saw this kid gaping,
Raised his milk chase to Zimmer's peachy face
And rolled out his complete smile
Before going off with friends
To leave Zimmer in that state of grace.

❧

A year later, Zimmer was renting rooms
From a woman named Tillie, who wanted
No jazz in her dank, unhallowed house.
Objecting even to lowest volume of solo piano,
She'd puff upstairs to bang on Zimmer's door.

Zimmer grew opaque and unwell,
Slouched to other apartments,
Begging to play records.
Duked, dePrezed, and unBased,
Longing for Billie, Monk, Brute, or Zoot,
He lived in silence through
That whole lost summer.

Aware of divine favor, he bided his time
Until his last night in Tillie's godless house,
Late—when he knew she was hard asleep—
He gave her the full "One O'clock Jump,"
Having Basie ride his horse of perfect time
Like an avenging angel over top volume,
Hoisting scotch and milk as he galloped
Into Tillie's ear, headlong down her throat
To roar all night in her sulfurous organs.

Dog Music

Amongst dogs are listeners and singers.
My big dog sang with me so purely,
puckering her ruffled lips into an O,
beginning with small, swallowing sounds
like Coltrane musing, then rising to power
and resonance, gulping air to continue—
her passion and sense of flawless form—
singing with me, but mostly for the art of dogs.

We joined in many fine songs—"Stardust,"
"Naima," "The Trout," "Jeg elsker Dig," "Perdido."
She was a great master and died young,
leaving me with unrelieved grief,
her talents known only to a few.

Now I have a small dog who does not sing
but listens with discernment, requiring
skill and spirit in my falsetto voice.
When I sing her name and words of love,
andante, con brio, vivace, adagio,
at times she is so moved she turns
to place her paw across her snout,
closing her eyes, sighing like a girl
I held and danced with years ago.

But I am a pretender to dog music.
Indeed, true strains rise only from
the rich, red chambers of a canine heart;
these melodies best when the moon is up,
listeners and singers together and apart,
beyond friendship and anger,

far from any human imposter—
songs of bones, turds, conquests,
hunts and scents, ballads of
long nights lifting to starlight.

in the Junior Baseball League in 1950.
Twice divorced, without children,
Howdy liked his Schlitz too much.
Our team was his only other pleasure,
but we were taking our licks
at the bottom of the standings,
embarrassed and blaming our manager.
Gus Thurman arranged a petition
for Howdy to be replaced and
brought it around to our houses.

Of course we won our next game.
Howdy was boisterous and thrilled.
After he thanked the umpire and
shook hands with the losing manager,
he turned with a smile to his team.

Just then—at that very moment—
Thurman handed him our petition.
Howdy read it carefully, studied all
our signatures. When finally he raised
his stricken face, we were all looking
at him from the bench, our mouths open
like a row of empty, baby swallows.

It was dusk and shadows were long.
Our girlfriends waited and watched,
their tawny legs crossed in the bleachers.
A distant freight, full from the mills,
whiffed its way through the switches
out of town. A covey of dirty wrappers

flapped up across the first base line.
The neon sign in the window
of the Cricket Bar and Grill
across the Eighth Street bridge
blinked once, then came on full.

The Light

I was a feverish, trembling child,
numb with illness and medicine.
A radiance of silver turning to blue
came through my window with
the smell of autumn leaf fires.
I thought this might be God's light
being swept by occasional bird flocks.
I had nothing else in my mind
or eye but this steadfast shining.

Many decades later, I nod in
my chair, and through the window
see leaves driving upward in the wind,
like ghosts of extinct birds
on their way to nowhere.

Then the aura of silver comes back,
turning to sky blue through the glass;
an old light that once had sustained me,
a new light that lets me slumber.

The Planets

I would step out with Grand-père Surmont from the back door of his
frame house in southern Indiana. In the summer night he smelled of salt
and grime. We'd step into his leek patch and look up together at the
stars.

Giddy with the immensity, I'd cling to his raspy miner's fingers and
ask him what he saw. In his heavy accent he'd tell me the names of
the planets and explain their places—*Pluton, Saturne, Mercure, Mars*—
how our earth was a planet, too, and we all circled the sun.

I fancy my hand in his made him remember his boyhood before he
ran away from conscription in France. Sometimes he'd tell me a little
of his sadness. Small, pale blue letters arrived each week, and I'd
fetch them from the mailbox for him. He read them eagerly but was
never able to afford a return, never saw his people again.

Now I step out from the house in Puivert and look up into French
skies, wondering what I have escaped. Grand-père, I am the age you
were when we stood together under the stars. I have had many
homes and lost the position of the planets. But this is my small
blue letter to you.

Amongst the French

I do not have their words,
do not have their years or customs.
Passing them on the road,
shy as fog passing down
slopes into the valley,
I always give first utterance
or make an uncertain gesture.

My neighbors are kind,
knowing I am like rain,
that if they wait long enough,
in time I will go away.

It is the same for me in
all directions—under stars
swarming out of foothills,
on the gravel I churn
with my shoes—east, west,
north, or south—the same.
If I remained in
this friendly place forever,
I would always be a stranger.

Love Poem

In southern France live two old horses,
High in the foothills, not even French,
But English, retired steeplechasers
Brought across to accept an old age
Of ambling together in the Pyrenees.
At times they whinny and kick
At one another with impatience,
But they have grown to love each other.

In time the gelding grows ill
And is taken away for treatment.
The mare pines, pokes at her food,
Dallies on her rides until the other
Comes home.
                        She is in her stall
When the trailer rumbles
Through the gate into the field,
And she sings with impatience
Until her door is opened.
                        Then full
Of sound and speed, in need of
Each other, they entwine their necks,
Rub muzzles, bumping flanks
To embrace in their own way.
Together they prance to
The choicest pasture,
Standing together and apart,
To be glad until
They can no longer be glad.

Unscathed

Cumbrous black-and-white cows,
At least thirty of them rumbling
Along the foothill path under
A cloudless, Pyrenean sky,
Spurred by a tiny French couple
Wielding burnished willow sticks;
Huge beasts munching and lowing
As they barge toward me.

I am paralyzed with senescence,
Not nimble enough to scramble
Up into the tall grass beside
The path.
            "Arrêt!" the farmers
Call to me, and so I freeze.

The ponderous cows are upon me,
Brush me by and nudge me
With their slobbery noses,
Breathing and moaning,
Copper bells dinning; their great
Hooves clomp like anvils
Within inches of my sneakers.
"Arrêt!" Oh yes. "Arrêt!"

When the herd has passed,
The minikin farmers, amused
Like sunflowers, come to me
And speak in inscrutable French:
"Well, monsieur," I suppose
They are saying. "That was close!

You did so well to be still.
And you are all right?"
                            I had
Thought it one of the most
Perilous moments of my life,
Ranking with close car wrecks,
Atomic blasts, near drownings,
Robberies, parking lot brawls—
Perhaps fifteen nervous tons of
Beast passing by me within inches.

My lungs flogged, my eyes crossed,
Yet here are *les petits fermiers*,
The adorable wife in flowered apron,
The husband in beret and vest,
Stroking my unscathed shoulder,
Smiling and shaking my hand,
As if to compliment me on my
Great good fortune—for being in
France on this winsome day.

What Zimmer Will Do

*The earliest color photographs were called autochromes
(1904–1930), formed on glass plates using a layer of minute
grains of starch dyed red, green, and blue coated with a
panchromatic emulsion. When viewed closely, the finished
images are like miniature Pointillist paintings. I am looking
at an image of two young French women sitting in a garden,*

and I become the great bird of love again;
crazy with spring, I swoop down
into the middle of the belle époque,
skitter and flop in the gravel path at the feet
of these two unsmiling French girls who sit
with their hair pulled back over eyes of shade.

I will make them blush and laugh
in their pink, summer frocks as I fly up
and dart between their wicker chairs
over beds of primroses, the fan plant
and columbines, to an open window of the house
where picnic hampers have been placed.

Then the three of us will ramble into
the sunlight and droning grasses,
and I will circle their lovely, oval heads,
gently pluck at their barrettes until
they laugh, "Zimmer, l'oiseau absurde!"
and toss me bits of bread and boiled egg.

This Small Woman

My vision is protracted
on the long road stretching
across the Plateau de Sault,
where the sweep of light
passes through my body
as if I do not exist.

Something moves in the distance.
It looks like a stork dragging
a ladder—then I realize
it is an old woman
pulling a clapboard cart.

Bent as the day moon,
she gathers sticks from
the roadside—come all the way
from the time of Charlemagne
to gather this load of fagot.

Desiderium

It begins as a sunlit ramble in
The Pyrenean foothills, but becomes
A dousing under reckless clouds.
Tall winds skid up from
The valley to fling aside my scarf
And clutch my heathen throat.
Wagtails and magpies sway
Overhead in slashing treetops,
Cursing me, the wind and rain,
As they watch the hell-bent sky for breaks.

In the nineteenth-century mountains,
Statues of the Son of God
Were crucified, nailed up
Naked and sallow along roadsides
To remind wayfarers in the clutch
Of such weather what
Suffering can really mean.

Medieval painters conceived church
Doctrine as weather in their murals:
Descending levels from glory to gloom—
Processions of sunlit saints and faithful
Treading high on clouds toward
A beckoning God; while beneath them
Prodigals and wastrels falter, naked
But still hopeful through cold rain;
And at bottom—on eye level
With the congregation—the damned
Are stewed in darkness, writhing
In a soup of vomit and feculence,

The devil and his henchmen
Crunching their bones forever.

In such weather one cannot demur.
When the sky has cleared
At last, I heave my sodden
Jacket over my shoulder
And head for loftier country,
Up a goat path in the foothills
Under pinewoods that open
In redolence to a high pasture.

I step out into the grass
Amidst butterflies and bees.
Having resolutely passed
Through wind and cold rain,
I give myself to brightness,
That I might somehow still join
The unfaltering sunlit parade
Of faithful moving toward God.

PART TWO   *Fifty Early Poems*

The Day Zimmer Lost Religion

The first Sunday I missed Mass on purpose
I waited all day for Christ to climb down
Like a wiry flyweight from the cross and
Club me on my irreverent teeth, to wade into
My blasphemous gut and drop me like
A red hot thurible, the devil roaring in
Reserved seats until he got the hiccups.

It was a long, cold way from the old days
When cassocked and surpliced I mumbled Latin
At the old priest and rang his obscure bell.
A long way from the dirty wind that blew
The soot like venial sins across the school yard
Where God reigned as a threatening
One-eyed triangle high in the fleecy sky.

The first Sunday I missed Mass on purpose
I waited all day for Christ to climb down
Like a playground bully, the cuts and mice
Upon his face agleam, and pound me
Till my irreligious tongue hung out.
But of course, He never came, knowing that
I was grown up and ready for Him now.

Zimmer in Grade School

In grade school I wondered
Why I had been born
To wrestle in the ashy puddles
With my square nose
Streaming mucus and blood,
My knuckles puffed from combat
And the old nun's ruler.
I feared everything: God,
Learning, and my schoolmates.
I could not count, spell, or read.
My report card proclaimed
These scarlet failures.
My parents wrung their loving hands.
My guardian angel wept constantly.

But I could never hide anything.
If I peed my pants in class
The puddle was always quickly evident,
My worst mistakes were at
The blackboard for Jesus and all
The saints to see.
                              Even now,
When I hide behind elaborate mask,
It is always known that I am Zimmer,
The one who does the messy papers
And fractures all his crayons,
Who spits upon the radiators
And sits all day in shame
Outside the office of the principal.

What Zimmer Would Be

When asked, I used to say,
"I want to be a doctor,"
Which is the same thing
As a child saying,
"I want to be a priest,"
Or
"I want to be a magician,"
Which is the laying on
Of hands, the vibrations,
The rabbit in the hat,
Or the body in the cup,
The curing of the sick
And the raising of the dead.

"Fix and fix, you're all better,"
I would say
To the neighborhood wounded
As we fought the world war
Through the vacant lots of Ohio.
"Fix and fix, you're all better,"
And they would rise
To fight again.
          But then
I saw my aunt die slowly of cancer
And a man struck down by a car.

All along I had really
Wanted to be a poet,
Which is, you see, almost
The same thing as saying,
"I want to be a doctor,"

"I want to be a priest,"
Or
"I want to be a magician."
All along, without realizing it,
I had wanted to be a poet.

Fix and fix, you're all better.

One for the Ladies at the Troy Laundry
Who Cooled Themselves for Zimmer

The ladies at the Troy Laundry pressed
And pressed in the warm fog of their labor.
They cooled themselves at the windows,
Steam rising from their gibbous skins
As I dawdled home from school.
In warmer weather they wore no blouses,
And if I fought the crumbling coke pile
To the top, they laughed and waved
At me, billowy from their irons.

Oh man, the ladies at the Troy Laundry
Smelled like codfish out of water,
And yet the very fur within their armpits
Made me rise wondering and small.

Zimmer Guilty of the Burnt Girl

Once a week
The burnt girl came peddling to our house,
Touching her sweet rolls with raisin fingers,
Her raw face struggling like a bubble
Through lava to say what she had
To sell and why: "Please buy my sweets
To mend my face."

Always I hid behind the piano and heard
My unflinching mother quietly buy a few,
And imagined apricots shriveling in sun,
Spiders boiling and dripping above matches.
Always when the burnt girl had gone,
I heard my mother drop her purchase
In the rubbish to be burned, and
I came out to see the pink graftings,
The horrid, sugared layers of the rolls.

I do not want
The burnt girl to come again.
I am guilty for her and of her.
Always in fever I think of that face.
Sometimes in love I believe that I am fire
Consuming myself, and the burnt girl
Suffers from my love as she sells
Her rolls to mend her face.

Father Animus and Zimmer

Father Animus asked who broke
The window in the sacristy.
I went head-on into evil,
Lying through my new incisors.

Holy Ghost moaned in my guts.
The light bulbs swayed on
Their cords in the parish
As each freckle on my face
Became a venial sin.

Father Animus asked his question.
My answer tangled in memories
Of ardor in the cozy parish:

How springtime I would swing up
Into dogwood trees in the churchyard,
Let the dark eyes of the blossoms read
Me like a breviary. Summertime
I ran the baselines as though
They were shadows of the spire.

In fall, exploring the attic
Of the old grade school,
I became my own history in
The dust, finding my father's
Initials carved in a broken desk,
My aunts' and uncles' first communions
Crumbling in antique records.

One winter, when the janitor
Had sprained his ankle, I climbed
Up inside the steeple to free
The tangled bell rope, rung after rung,
Through drafts and timberings.
Bats retreated, wind screeched
Outside through the slate shingles.

I felt I was rising in the head of
Father Animus, through warnings
And pronouncements, his strict,
Reluctant love diminishing as
I aspired, choked, deprived
Of space as I climbed higher.

Father Animus asked who
Broke the sacristy window,
And the cross on the spire,
Tucking in its legs,
Flew away in sorrow.

A Zimmershire Lad

Oh, what a lad was Zimmer
    Who would rather swill than think,
Who grew to fat from trimmer,
    While taking ale to drink.

Now his stomach hangs so low
    And now his belt won't hook,
Now his cheeks go to and fro
    When he leaps across a brook.

Oh lads, ere your flesh decay,
    And your sight grow dimmer,
Beware the ale foam in your way
    Or you will end like Zimmer.

An Enzyme Poem for Suzanne

What a drag it must be for you!
I slog along, ignoring you like my heart beat.
I gurgle and mold like an old fruit cellar,
Then suddenly you'll walk through a door
And foam me like ancient cider in heat.
Then I'll fall all about you, blathering
With lost time, making you numb with words,
Wanting to mix our molecules, trying
To tell you of weeks in fifteen minutes.
Sometimes you must wonder what the hell
It is with Zimmer.
                                This is to tell you
That you are my enzymes, my yeast,
All the things that make my cork go pop.

Zimmer Envying Elephants

I have a wide, friendly face
Like theirs, yet I can't hang
My nose like a fractured arm
Nor flap my dishpan ears.
I can't curl my canine teeth,
Swing my tail like a filthy tassel,
Nor make thunder without lightning.

But I'd like to thud amply around
For a hundred years or more,
Stuffing an occasional tree top
Into my mouth, screwing hugely for
Hours at a time, gaining weight,
And slowly growing a few hairs.

Once in a while I'd charge a power pole
Or smash a wall down just to keep
Everybody loose and at a distance.

Zimmer Loathing the Gentry

Their faces are like fine watches
Insinuating jewels.
Their movements can buy or sell you.
When the legs of the gentry dance for charity,
Meat splashes in the soups of the poor.
The eyes of the gentry are polished and blown;
When they look at you, you are worthless.
The gentry protect their names like hymens,
They suck their names like thumbs,
But they sign their names and something happens.
While, Zimmer, I can write, Zimmer,
All day, and nothing happens.

Zimmer's Bed

Old bed, you are a garden.
Each night I roll over
And sink through you
Like a root into
Darkness. Now I will
Say goodnight, goodnight.
I have slept on you
So long I forget
How much I love you.
Yet my children and poems
Are sewn in you.
Can you tell me
If they will bloom
And be immortal?
Never mind. Goodnight,
Goodnight.

Wanda Being Beautiful

To be beautiful is to somehow keep
A dozen fires burning at night,
To know that all eyes shining
Out of the trees are afraid of you.
It is to know that every crackle of
A twig, every footfall is a threat,
That desire is greatest from a distance.

To be beautiful is to stay on the move
Through every season, to watch sharply
As you take what you want, but mostly
It is knowing how to choose dry wood,
How to bank your fires against cold.

Lester Tells of Wanda and the Big Snow

Some years back I worked a strip mine
Out near Tylersburg. One day it starts
To snow and by two we got three feet.
I says to the foreman, "I'm going home."
He says, "Ain't you stayin' till five?"
I says, "I got to see to my cows,"
Not telling how Wanda was there at the house.
By the time I make it home at four
Another foot is down and it don't quit
Until it lays another. Wanda and me
For three whole days seen no one else.
We tunneled the drifts and slid
Right over the barbed wire, laughing
At how our heartbeats melted the snow.
After a time the food was gone and I thought
I'd butcher a cow, but then it cleared
And the moon come up as sweet as an apple.
Next morning the ploughs got through. It made us sad.
It don't snow like that no more. Too bad.

Robyn Hode and Maid Wanda

In somer, when the shawes be sheyne,
　　And wodes do sprytly ryng,
Hit is so mery in the leves
　　To here the briddis syng.

A yeman lyved amidst these trees,
　　By name of Robyn Hode,
A prode and mery outlaw he,
　　Yet full of certaine gude.

One day he boed an arrow
　　Depe in to a grene wode tree,
But Robyn nere fell don when
　　The swete barke cryde, "Ah me!"

For in the holowe of the tree
　　A wench hae hidde herself,
The yeman to ploke his arow back
　　Wode hae gie al his pelf.

Robyn toke her up from thair
　　And bond her wunde sae sorre,
He loked upon her wyth gladde eye
　　For she was fare and morre.

Now in the grene wode do they lyve
　　With lytel Johnn, Scarloke, and Monke,
Mony a wondrous tyme hae they hadde,
　　Ful many more shaftes hae been sonke.

Dear Wanda (Letter from Rollo)

Dear Wanda,
A month ago the sun disappeared.
Clouds swelled up like giant fungi.
I figured something big was up
So I tore the old barn down
And built myself a ponderous raft,
Hoisting the house to put on top.
I laid in a hundred cases of Stroh's,
Then I gathered animals two by two:
The sweet swine and foul goats,
Cattle to breathe me some peace.
I went a long way for alligators—
Mountain lions ate the sheep before
I could get them in. Two turtles,
Two hares in heat, two tree frogs,
And a pair of rutting reindeer.
The snow geese boarded each other
In anticipation of their nest!
Wanda, I had big plans for us as well.
But as the rain began to fall
I could not find you anywhere.
Water's up to my armpits now,
Buffalo and plough horses kick
Boards right out of my keel.
Termites gnaw at the strakes.
But why should I give a damn?
Wanda, where the hell were you?
        Still fondly,
        Rollo

Thurman Dreaming in Right Field

In right field I am so far out
The batter has unwound before
I hear the crack of his effort,
And the ball whirrs out and bounces
Like the wind off the wall
At idiot angles.
                I am lonely
In that distance.
                  The moon shines
Like a long fly in right field
Where rain falls first
And snow drifts in winter.
Sun cuts intricate shadows from
The decks above my head
And balls, dropping like duck hawks,
Suddenly grow dull in the broken light
Of right field.
                But there is
Always time for dreaming before
The impossible catch, the wheel-
And-shotgun throw on one bounce to
The plate, where the catcher slams
The ball onto the sliding runner's thigh,
And the crowd goes roaring, "Thurman!"
In that far field where
I am dreaming once again.

Thurman's Slumping Blues

One day out in right field
The ball went by me quicker
Than a flushed-out quail.
I wagged my glove at it
But what I got was wind.
Then I fell down like a fool.
Fans stung me harder than
A swarm of bald-faced hornets.
That was what started
The whole damned thing.

I felt the sap run out of my knees,
Looked at my hands, they smelled of fish.
Wanda was up there in the box seats,
Sitting on a whole school of mackerel.

We dropped in the standings.
Pitchers pulled the string
And tied me up in knots.
I went left when I should have gone right.
Wanda commenced to acting skittish.
Today I woke up and she was gone.
Over my steak and eggs
The paper tells me that
This is last place.

Someone Points and Says, Up There's Old Thurman

in the bleachers. But I am half asleep,
spread-eagle on the planks. Right field
stretches away from me like a pasture
with the gate open. Across the green on
the diamond, infielders chatter and prance
as they snap the ball around like a dragonfly.
They think they will live forever.
This is the saddest thing I know.

Here I am, not far away, prisoner in my skin
and slow bones, murmuring to myself,
dreaming of towels, leather, jockstraps,
wet socks draped over locker doors—
or I am running down the long tunnel
from the dressing room to the field,
my spikes clattering on cement,
but no matter now hard I run,
I never get to the grass.

Irene Gogle

Bugs lived in her hair.
Her one dress was weary.
The nuns were kind
But kept their distance.
When she read aloud
The tedious clock ticked
Between her words.

"Go-go!" we called her.
"Go-go is your girlfriend!"
—when we wished to insult
Another boy. I loathed her
Aloud with the rest;
Once, on a dare, pushed
Her into a classmate so
He could feel her breasts.
The nun broke a yardstick
Over our cowering backs.

On the playground she would
Stand alone by the fence,
Bouncing a dirty tennis ball,
Pretending to be cheerful.

Why should she come to
My mind again? I say words
To my grade-school son:
Kindness, love, compassion.
I pray to God for definitions.

The Eisenhower Years

Flunked out and laid off,
Zimmer works for his father
At Zimmer's Shoes for Women.
The feet of old women awaken
From dreams, they groan and rub
Their hacked-up corns together;
At last they stand and walk
Downtown to Zimmer's fitting stool
Where he talks to the feet,
Reassures them with
Blissful ties in medium heels.

Home from work he checks the mail
For greetings from his draft board.
After supper he listens to Brubeck,
Lays out with a tumbler of Thunderbird,
Cigarettes and *From Here to Eternity.*

That evening he goes out to the bars,
Drinks three pitchers of Stroh's,
Ends up in the wee hours leaning
On a lamp post, his tie loosened,
Fedora pushed back on his head,
A Chesterfield stuck to his lips.

All of complacent America
Spreads around him in the night.
Nothing is moving in this void,
Only the feet of old women,
Twitching and shuffling in pain.

Zimmer sighs and takes a drag,
Exhales through his nostrils.
He knows nothing and feels little.
He has never been anywhere
And fears where he is going.

The Duke Ellington Dream

Of course Zimmer was late for the gig.
Duke was pissed and growling at the piano,
But Jeep, Brute, Rex, Cat, and Cootie
All moved down on the chairs
As Zimmer walked in with his tenor.
Everyone knew that the boss had arrived.

Duke slammed out the downbeat for "Caravan"
And Zimmer stood up to take his solo.
The whole joint suddenly started jiving,
Chicks came up to the bandstand
To hang their lovelies over the rail.
Duke was sweating but wouldn't smile
Through chorus after chorus after chorus.

It was the same with "Satin Doll,"
"Do Nothing till You Hear from Me,"
"Warm Valley," "In a Sentimental Mood";
Zimmer blew them so they would stay played.

After the final set he packed
His horn and was heading out
When Duke came up and collared him.
"Zimmer," he said. "You most astonishing ofay!
You have shat upon my charts,
But I love you madly."

The Great House

Over and over it happens: my wife and I are
Out walking, we come to a great stone house
Built into a hillside. We are young again;
All things seem possible on this perfect day.
Suddenly we know that the house is ours!
We enter in joy, exulting in all we own:
Circular staircases, niches, ballrooms,
A dozen rooms full of leather-bound books,
Lace curtains, puppet theatres, daguerreotypes,
Chests full of doilies and ancient manuscripts,
Hand printing presses, bowls of potpourri;
There are antique cribs, rocking chairs,
A canopied bed. We could start our lives again!
All windows swing open to singing birds and trees
Through which we see a whitewashed, sunlit city.

At night, after a lingering dinner and wine,
Lieder and string quartets by candle glow,
We ascend the tower, open the skylight,
And turn the huge reflector into position.
The shimmer that we see has traveled for eons.
Under the circling stars, the birds against
The moon, with the vast rooms breathing
Beneath us, we know that the only sadness
In the world will be to leave this house.

A Final Affection

I love the accomplishments of trees,
How they try to restrain great storms
And pacify the very worms that eat them.
Even their deaths seem to be considered.

I fear for trees, loving them so much.
I am nervous about each scar on bark,
Each leaf that browns. I want to
Lie in their crotches and sigh,
Whisper of sun and rains to come.

Sometimes on summer evenings I step
Out of my house to look at trees
Propping darkness up to the silence.

When I die I want to slant up
Through those trunks so slowly
I will see each rib of bark, each whorl;
Up through the canopy, the subtle veins
And lobes touching me with final affection;
Then to hover above and look down
One last time on the rich upliftings,
The circle that loves the sun and moon,
To see at last what held the darkness up.

When Angels Came to Zimmer

One morning a great gaggle slid
Down through holes in clouds,
Twirling like maple seeds
Through trees to the window screen.
Fervent as new tussock moths,
They flapped and dashed themselves,
Smearing their heavenly dust,
Until Zimmer, in pity and alarm,
Opened to let them into his study.
They flew in with smiles and sighs,
Making him bashful, as if a dozen
Gorgeous chorus girls had suddenly
Pranced into the room.
                              They perched on
Bookshelves, cigar stubs, and beer cans;
One even tried to sit on Zimmer's lap.
All day they danced the lindy,
And some, not knowing better, dabbled
Their darling toes in the toilet bowl.
They sang chorus after chorus of
"Stardust" and "Moonlight in Vermont,"
Constantly touching and stroking Zimmer.
Then at day's end, as if someone
Had rung a bell, they stood to sing
A final chorus of "Deep Purple."
With a whoosh of air and expensive perfume,
They fluttered from the room and ascended.
Zimmer stepped out to watch them rise
And flapped his soiled hankie at the stars.

Work

To have done it thirty years
Without question! Yet I tell myself
I am grateful for all work;
At noon in my air-conditioned office
With a sandwich and a poem,
I try to recollect nature;
But a clerk comes in with papers
To be signed. I tell myself
The disruption does not matter;
It is all work. Computer runs,
Contracts, invoices, poems, the same
As breaking shells, hunting woods,
Making pots, or gathering grain.
Jazzmen even refer to sex as work.
Some primitive people believe
That death is work. When my wife asks
What I am doing, I always answer,
I am working, working, working.

Now I know I will spend the rest
Of my life trying for perfect work,
A work as rare as aurora borealis,
So fine it will make all other work
Seem true, one that will last as long
As words will last. At home
In my room, I mumble to myself
Over my poems; over supper I talk
To myself; as I carpenter or paint
Or carry the groceries up the steps,
I am speaking words to myself.
"What are you doing?" my children ask.
I am working, working, working.

Zimmer Imagines Heaven

I sit with Joseph Conrad in Monet's garden.
We are listening to Yeats chant his poems,
A breeze stirs through Thomas Hardy's moustache,
John Skelton has gone to the house for beer,
Wanda Landowska lightly fingers a harpsichord,
Along the spruce-tree walk Roberto Clemente and
Thurman Munson whistle a baseball back and forth.
Mozart chats with Ellington in the roses.

Monet smokes and dabs his canvas in the sun,
Brueghel and Turner set easels behind the wisteria.
The band is warming up in the Big Studio:
Bean, Brute, Bird, and Serge on saxes;
Kai, Bill Harris, Lawrence Brown trombones;
Little Jazz, Clifford, Fats, Diz on trumpets;
Klook plays drums; Mingus bass; Bud the piano.
Later Madam Schuman-Heink will sing Schubert,
The monks of Benedictine Abbey will chant.
There will be more poems from Emily Dickinson,
James Wright, John Clare, Walt Whitman.
Shakespeare rehearses players for *King Lear*.

At dusk Alice Toklas brings out platters
Of sweetbreads, Salad Livoniére,
And a tureen of Gazpacho of Málaga.
After the meal Brahms passes fine cigars.
God comes then, radiant with a bottle of cognac,
She pours generously into the snifters,
I tell Her I have begun to learn what
Heaven is about. She wants to hear.
It is, I say, being thankful for eternity.
Her smile is the best part of the day.

The Origins of Love

The first time I saw her, light was falling,
Air was rich like the last days of autumn.
Despite her dazzle and warmth, I was melancholy,
As I have always been in the presence of beauty.

From then on I tried every day to be decent.
When I was crass, her lovely shoulders
Drooped like tulips in the garden.
I did not want to wait, and yet I waited
As I had never done before, and surely
In time the delicate snow began to fall.

So the glory of my restraint inspired me.
I became eloquent, attentive, civilized.
Times I had to say goodbye to her became
The greatest burdens of my onerous life.

Although she gave me no reason to doubt,
I was constantly afraid; I thought perhaps
A god might come and take her from me.
Somehow it pleased me that others admired her,
Yet it made my knuckles
Turn white like worried children.

The Sounds of Magpie

Nobody ever owned magpie,
But now he is down in the berm.
His friends hold raucous wake
Above him before they drift away.
Magpie needs no undertaker,
Has always been dressed for the end.

Magpie attempted to live a good life,
Built well and saved bright things he loved.
He tried speaking gently to his children,
But forever ended saying, raw-raw-raw!

He loved his mate and chased with her,
Kissed her with a clack when they met;
As they made love he'd go, aw-aw-aw!

Magpie would get sick with the drink;
He picked dead flesh off an old cow's back,
Flew to a tree and threw up, aargh!

When magpie was young he said, now-now-now!
When he grew old he gargled with glass,
Ground his beak and said, fuck you, fuck you!

Magpie grew quiet, knew something was up;
He let the young birds chatter and chase.
One day he went to feed on the road;
When he got smacked he said, oof!

The Old Trains at Night

In the forties and fifties
It seemed like every time trains
Hauled out of town at night,
They rolled into my flawless sleep.
Awake, I loved to watch them come in
Like big dogs breathing hard,
Grinding their cheeks at the stations.

Then the first diesels came through,
Piddling on crossties and smelling of crap.
The damned things bred like dingy rabbits
Till by 1960 all the real trains were scrap.
Now the world belongs to bloodless bastards
Who tell us all the steam trains are gone.

But on rainy nights I still hear them
Mope around, mumble to themselves,
Slipping on glazed rails and belching.
I wake to hear them hooting at
Each other over forlorn distances,
And I start pulling for them, too.

They were finest in winter when
They showed what they could do,
Slamming their way through huge drifts,
Chests heaving and great hearts pounding.

But they ran best on moonlight,
Heaving out steam to secret wildflowers,
Sliding through ground fog
As they hauled themselves
Panting into our dreams.

Yellow Sonnet

Zimmer no longer wishes to write
About the dimming of his lights,
Recounting all his small terrors.
Instead he tells of brilliance,
Walking home from first grade
In springtime, light descending
To hold itself and dazzle him
In an outburst of dandelions.
It was then he learned that
He would always love yellow,
Its warm dust on his knuckles,
The memory of gathering pieces
To carry home in his lunch pail
As a love gift for his mother.

Sitting with Lester Young

Dusk must become your light
If you want to see Lester Young.
So Zimmer sits beside him at
His window in the Alvin Hotel.
Pres is blue beyond redemption.
His tenor idle on the table,
He looks down at the street,
Drinking his gin and port.

Buildings slice the last light
From the day. If Pres could
Shuffle into a club again like
A wounded animal, he would
Blow his ultimate melancholy,
But nights belong to others now.
Zimmer can only watch Pres
In the half-light of his sadness,
Old whispers slipping around,
Hinting words into melodies,
As holy silence means the most.

The Tenth Circle

Dear Dad,
Do not fall for the third time,
Or if you do, tell no one.
Hunch over your agony and
Make it your ultimate secret.
You have done this before.
Shrug, tell a joke, go on.
If an ambulance slips up
Quietly to the back door,
Do not get on. They mean to
Take you to the tenth circle
Where everyone is turned in
One direction, piled like cordwood
Inside the cranium of Satan
So that only the light of
Television shines in their eyes.
Dad, call if you need help,
But do not let them take you
Easily to this place where
They keep the motor idling
On the long black car, where if
Someone cries out in the night
Only the janitor comes.
                    Love,
                    Paul

The Place

Once in your life you pass
Through a place so pure
It becomes tainted even
By your regard, a space
Of trees and air where
Dusk comes as perfect ripeness.
Here the only sounds are
Sighs of rain and snow,
Small rustlings of plants
As they unwrap in twilight.
This is where you will go
At last when coldness comes.
It is something you realize
When you first see it,
But instantly forget.
At the end of your life
You remember and dwell in
Its faultless light forever.

The Great Bird of Love

I want to become a great night bird
Called The Zimmer, grow intricate gears
And tendons, brace my wings on updrafts,
Roll them down with a motion
That lifts me slowly into the stars
To fly above the troubles of the land.
When I soar the moon will shine past
My shoulder and slide through
Streams like a luminous fish.
I want my cry to be huge and confident,
The undefiled movement of my wings
To fold and unfold on rising gloom.

People will see my silhouette from
Their windows and be comforted,
Knowing that, though oppressed,
They are cherished and watched over,
Can turn to kiss their children,
Tuck them into their beds and say:
    Sleep tight.
    No harm tonight.
    In starry skies
    The Zimmer flies.

The Persistence of Fatherhood

Yesterday the autumn finished.
I began raking it into piles
Around the house. Sue came out
And called from the distance.
I cupped my ears but could not hear
Through bare winds and branches rattling.

I thought she said,
"Your father's on the phone,"
And started walking toward
The house, until I remembered
He's been dead a dozen years.

Then last night this dream:
Suddenly leaves were children's clothing,
Blue jeans, caps, and flannel shirts.
I raked them up, bent over by sadness,
Fatherhood all used up and gone,
Playthings and story times gone,
I swept and piled, doing my duties,
Only this caretaking left to do.

What I Know about Owls

They can break the night like glass.
They can hear a tick turn over
In the fur of a mouse thirty acres away.
Their eyes contain a tincture of magic
So potent they see cells dividing in
The hearts of their terrified victims.
You cannot hear their dismaying who,
You cannot speak their fearsome name
Without ice clattering in your arteries.

But in daytime owls rest in blindness,
Their liquids no longer boiling.
There is a legend that if you are careful
And foolishly ambitious, you can approach
Them and stroke for luck and life
The feathers on their foreheads,
Risking always that later on some
Quiet night when you least expect it
The owl, remembering your transgression,
Will slice into your lamplight like a razor,
Bring you down splayed from your easy chair,
Your ribcage pierced, organs raked
From their nests, and your head slowly
Rolling down the owl's bloody throat
Into the fierce acids of its stomach.

A Romance for the Wild Turkey

They are so cowardly and stupid
Indians would not eat them
For fear of assuming their qualities.

The wild turkey always stays close
To home, flapping up into trees
If alarmed, then falling out again.
When shot it explodes like a balloon
Full of blood. It bathes by grinding
Itself in coarse dirt, is incapable
Of passion or anger, knows only
Vague innocence and extreme caution,
Walking around in underbrush
Like a cantilevered question mark,
Retreating at least hint of danger.

I hope when the wild turkey
Dreams at night it flies high up
In gladness under vast islands
Of mute starlight, its silhouette
Vivid in the full moon, guided always
By radiant configurations, high
Over chittering fields of corn
And the trivial fires of men,
Never to land again nor be regarded
As fearful, stupid, and unsure.

The Brain of the Spider

Imagine a spider's brain,
The various colored segments of its matter:
Crimson for power, blue for balance,
Green for judgment, yellow for cunning.
Think how it inspires the shape of dew,
How it squares frost and causes
The silver sweep of its filaments
To stroke your face in woods and streets.
Regard the air it fixes between strands,
Its careful allowances for time and space.
Then consider what is most complex:
The unnerving grayness of its patience,
White speed of its sudden charges,
The raven segment it maintains for death.

But Bird

Some things you should forget,
But Bird was something to believe in.
Autumn '54, twenty, drafted,
Stationed near New York for training,
En route to atomic tests in Nevada,
I taught myself to take
A train to Pennsylvania Station,
Walk up Seventh to Fifty-second Street,
Looking for music and legends.
One night I found the one
I wanted. Bird.

Five months later no one was brave
When the numbers ran out.
All equal—privates and colonels—
Down on our knees in the slits
As the voice counted backward
In the dark turning to light.

But "Charlie Parker" it said
On the Basin Street marquee,
And I dug for the cover charge,
Sat down in the cheap seats.
He slumped in from the kitchen,
Powder blue serge and suedes.
No jive Bird, he blew crisp and clean,
Bringing each face in the crowd
Gleaming to the bell of his horn.
No fluffing, no wavering,
But soaring like on my old
Verve waxes back in Ohio.

Months later, down in the sand,
The bones in our fingers were
Suddenly x-rayed by the flash.
We moaned together in light
That entered everything,
Tried to become the earth itself
As the shock rolled toward us.

But Bird. I sat through three sets,
Missed the last train out,
Had to bunk in a roach pad,
Sleep in my uniform, almost AWOL.
But Bird was giving it all away,
One of his last great gifts,
And I was there with my
Rosy cheeks and swan neck,
Looking for something to believe in.

When the trench caved in it felt
Like death, but we clawed out,
Walked beneath the roiling, brutal cloud
To see the flattened houses,
Sheep and pigs blasted,
Ravens and rabbits blind,
Scrabbling in the grit and yucca.

But Bird. Remember Bird.
Five months later he was dead,
While I was down on my knees,
Wretched with fear in
The cinders of the desert.

Romance

This frightened, horny boy
Sits in a jazz club full of
Jungle ferns and leopard skins.

A piano trio is playing,
Dulcet and precise,
"My One and Only Love."

Hank Jones or Billy Taylor?
Al Haig? Ellis Larkins?
It does not matter.

What counts is this song
About something we do not even
Presume to hope for anymore.

Just in time, this wistful,
Tipsy boy hears about love
So sure it lasts a lifetime.

The Existential Year

I read the first three pages
    of the introduction to
        Being and Nothingness a dozen times.

I incessantly searched
    the streets for a woman
        who looked like Juliette Greco.

I learned to pronounce
    the word "Heidegger." I wore
        my coat on my shoulders

and long scarves, which twisted
    agonizingly in the wind.
        I always looked

as if I were about
    to barf up my brains.
        I vowed I would never

look backward or forward,
    knowing that Being
        was enough In-itself.

The Beautiful Ethiopian Navy

Having grown up far from the sea,
My friends didn't lightly heave-to
And go yo-ho-ho. These were men
Of the brush and distant peaks,
Young, reedy, black, intense,
They smoked unfiltered cigarettes
And drank straight rum.
Women turned to watch us pass,
Them in their crisp whites,
Me in my rumpled jacket and tie—
Negash, Maconan, Tassew, Seifu,
And Zimmer, like a rolling garden
Of dahlias and one elated lily.

Never have I had such friends again.
Brothers we declared ourselves,
Teaching songs to each other
And stories, how to throw spears
And footballs in Golden Gate Park,
Arguing games, books, religion,
In the bars of San Francisco.

As I have remembered them,
Please do not tell me they are all
Likely gone, my beautiful fellows
From Asmara, Gondar, Harar, Diredawa,
Wandering parched lands of famine
And dying with the animals, or finished
In the bloody spray of politics.

Forty years ago I watched them sail
Away to the other side of the world.
I have not had such friends again.

The Weathers of Love

1

Outdoors all day with you
In weather that cracks
Our small ear bones and drives
Rain through stones,
Snapping our coats like sails,
Suddenly in late afternoon
The scud is swallowed by blue.
Tiny flowers unwrap in sunlight,
Moss begins to passion.
So we have done it again,
Walked all day to love.

2

Today there was light sifting
Of snow from a joyless sky,
No great burden, but something
For us to bear up under.
Tonight we count on nothing.
The house begins cracking,
Big dogs moan on their rugs,
Pipes grow cold and indifferent,
Chill slips into our knuckles.
Twenty false steps outdoors in
The frigid, hard edges of this air would
Shiver us, so we hold each other
And give the fire everything it needs.

3

You swat a sunlit cabbage moth
With your white baseball cap,
Shouting and flinging organic dust.

The garden goes on contending
With itself, great heads wrap and tighten,
Vines quietly pump up their fruits,
Vegetables sit on their secrets.

Still you imagine perfection
And fear the gnawing worm.
I cheer you on,
Get that bastard!
I fall in love some more.

4

What to say to our children
Of our long time
In the weathers of love?

That it was never what we predicted,
But what we learned in time.

That to see you waving to me
From a hazy distance is as precious
As holding you in my arms.

That sometimes on a rainy day
Just knowing you are
In the next room saves my life.

Love Poem

1

Last days before first frost
we stroll out hand in hand
to see yellow sulfurs lift
in multitudes
over the fields
flittering in ecstatic pairs
to descend
and spangle the hay

2

Months later
trudging winter fields
in the morning sun
we see their million
rapturous spirits have risen
through layers of drift
to glitter
on the snow crust

Big Blue Train

The big blue train coughs,
coughs again, and is silent,
then resolves itself and slams
its pistons down once more.

They stroke three times, sighing
and blowing, then stagger cold.
Next time they bluster once,
hold the cycle and gather fire.

Fire on fire, and the engine
heats up glowing on the tracks.
It hisses, tensing its wheel rods,
impatient to connect its gears.

Clouds of steam and black smoke
billow up to the station canopy,
slip along the filthy girders,
and curtain out to the sky.

Zimmer pulls the whistle cord
and cleaves the chill air in two.
Doors are slamming, signals flash,
people kiss on the concourse.

He taps the gritty meters,
eases slowly up on the brake
and brings the throttle down—
the engine knocks and heaves.

A long, echoing chain of thunder,
then the big blue train inches
forward out of the station,
creaking and swinging its lanterns,

slides into the early dawn,
through lighted grids of the city,
faces in its windows growing
vague in the rising light.

The Books

The printed word is part of a vestigial order
we are moving away from.
—SVEN BERKERTS

The first time you opened one—
Pages winging lightly as you turned,
Making delicate, puffing scrolls
Of air, aroma of paper
And ink feathering your nostrils—
You knew the rest of your life
Would be part of their singular flights,
Vast flocks, brave migrations.

Now recall their variety.
Fragile volumes fanning at cusps
Of flowers. Tomes bursting
Out of meadows when alarmed.
Earth books, star books, sea books,
Some that mutter to themselves,
Scratching earnestly for seeds,
Others that clang and strike like
Thunderbolts out of the sky's core—
Yet such forlorn creatures in the end,
Hunched over, swaying back and forth,
With light seeping out of their eyes.
They disappear like ancient magic,
Like phantoms of lost animals
Or ghosts of chestnuts and elms.

Before the Moon Came Up Last Night

We walked on the old road
That is crossed by the Milky Way.
Suddenly the hill's silhouette
Erupted in squalling and growls,
A swirl of deadly encounter
Raging on and on and on,
Until it faded into
The dimming trees.

This morning we found remains
Of slaughter: drifting turkey feathers,
Frantic scribbles of retreat,
Blood drops burning in old snow.

Tonight at dusk coyotes sing
Back and forth from woods
To woods—folks songs of triumph
And sweetness, perhaps,
Or ancient Arabic melodies.
Here I am, they say, There you are,
We've slept well and made love,
Now we must hunt again.

I imagine them tugging
The sunset back and forth,
Eyes crimson with happiness,
Tongues lolling out of their mouths,
Heads thrown back so far
If you were the moon,
You could look straight down
The shafts of their throats
To see the proud, glowing hearts.

Suck It Up

Two pugs on the undercard step through
The ropes in satin robes,
Pink Adidas with tassels,
Winking at the women in the crowd.
At instructions they stare down hard
And refuse to touch their gloves,
Trying to make everyone believe
That this will be a serious dustup.

But when the bell rings they start
Slapping like a couple of Barbie dolls.
One throws a half-hearted hook,
The other flicks out his jab,
They bounce around for a while
Then grab each other for a tango.
The crowd gets tired of booing
And half of them go out for beer,
But I've got no place to hide.

A week after a cancer scare,
A year from a detached retina,
Asthmatic, overweight, trickling,
Drooling, bent like a blighted elm
In my pajamas and slippers,
I have tuned up my hearing aids to sit in
Numbness without expectation before
These televised Tuesday Night Fights.

With a minute left in the fourth,
Scuffling, they butt their heads
By accident. In midst of the catcalls
And hubbub suddenly they realize

How much they hate each other.
They start hammering and growling,
Really dealing, whistling combinations,
Hitting on the breaks and thumbing.
At last one guy crosses a stiff jab
With a roundhouse right and the other
Loses his starch. The guy wades into
The wounded one, pounding him
Back and forth until he goes down,
Bouncing his head on the canvas.

The count begins, but he is saved
By the bell and his trainers haul
Him to his stool as the lens zooms in.

I come to the edge of my La-Z-Boy,
Blinking and groaning from my incision,
Eager for wise, insightful instruction.

He gets a bucket of water in his face,
A sniff on the salts while the cutman
Tries to close his wounds with glue.
His nose is broken, eyes are crossed,
His lips bleed like two rare steaks.
His cornermen take turns slapping his cheeks.
"Suck it up!" they shout.
Suck it up.

Passage

Years ago, walking home from classes,
I came upon an old black couple
hunched down on the sidewalk over
the mangled corpse of their dog.

The woman swayed above the body,
her shoulders quaking with misery;
the man had his hand on her back.

I stood in silence beside their grief,
looking down at his worn jacket,
her sweater spattered with blood.

Finally, because I had no experience,
I imagined that words might serve:
"You'll have to get her another dog."

For a long time I listened to the throb
of her weeping, to traffic
sucking wind in the oily street.
My bones grew brittle as I waited.

At last the man drew his answer
heavily up from the deep, "That's all right,"
he said. "You go on along. It's our sadness."

In Apple Country

A year begins with marriage in apple country,
Immaculate drift of lace in light crosswinds,
Consummation of dusts, caverns of blossoms,
Endless circles forming and expanding.

As a child I drew circles for hours,
Arcing the compass around its point
To feel the pleasure of circumference,
Roundness conjoined, swallowing, embracing,
Shoebox full of buckeyes in their husks,
Baseballs, acorns, bags of marbles,
Tulip bulbs, yo-yo's, dandelions—
But ripe apples sliced across always
Made the most perfect circles of all.

Late in harvest good pickers wear gloves
To keep their fingertips from frostbite,
The delicate twist and pluck—
A hundred and fifty bushels a day.

Do apples die when they are picked?
When they tumble from baskets and bags,
Bruised, crushed, slithering under boot soles?
When the first bite is taken,
Sweet death dribbling onto the chin?

In truth they triumph and abide.
If all the apples ripening
One fall day and all the circles
Ever grown in these orchards
Draped across the driftless hills

Were counted by a great master,
They would total the number of stars
In western skies on an autumn night.

I lean back in my garden chair and watch
The great harvests turn slowly in vast distances—
Red, yellow, green, their blemishes and tiny wormholes
Revolving in the October sky all the way
Out to the round ends of the universe.

Acknowledgments

The author and publisher gratefully acknowledge the following journals in which some of the poems in the section "Twenty-three New Poems" originally appeared: *Brilliant Corners, Chariton Review, Denver Quarterly, Field, Georgia Review, Gettysburg Review, Great River Review, Iowa Review, New Letters, Poetry,* and *Prairie Schooner.* Some of these poems appear here in slightly altered forms.

Poems in the section "Fifty Early Poems" were selected from *Crossing to Sunlight: Selected Poems,* by Paul Zimmer (Athens: University of Georgia Press, 1996), now out of print.

DEDICATIONS
"The Moment" to Justine Zimmer, "Irene Gogle" to Erik Zimmer, "Zimmer Imagines Heaven" to Merrill Leffler, "The Old Trains at Night" to Gary Gildner, and "Sitting with Lester Young" to Michael S. Harper.